T'ALKING B✺LL✺CKS!

TOTALLY STUPID EVERYDAY REMARKS

PROFESSOR R. LINGO

Crombie Jardine
PUBLISHING LIMITED

Crombie Jardine
PUBLISHING LIMITED
Office 2, 3 Edgar Buildings
George Street
Bath
BA1 2FJ
www.crombiejardine.com

Published by Crombie Jardine Publishing Limited
First edition, 2008
Copyright © 2008,
Crombie Jardine Publishing Limited

ISBN 978-1-906051-18-1

Written by Alan Oliver
Cover illustration by Paul Palmer
Designed by www.glensaville.com
Printed and bound in Great Britain by
Polestar UK Print Limited - Wheatons division

CONTENTS

PROLOGUE

This is a study and analysis of our great language and the things we all say that, when you think about it (as opposed to when you don't think about it), make no sense whatsoever. It is a collection of clichés and the tried and trusted sayings we trot out, often without even thinking, almost with a kind of reflex reaction. Whilst some sayings may bear a resemblance to grammatical correctness, unfortunately, strict interpretation takes them totally out of context and renders many of our favourite sayings total bollocks.

Imagine, if you will, that you are an alien from another planet (why did I add that?) and your mission is to assume human form and mingle with us. You might just need a little pre-mission training to even try and begin to get your little green head around the utter rubbish we spout daily.

If we bump into someone (buzz… factual error unless one or both is blind) we know in a far off place, and one of us doesn't say "It's a small world!" it's a minor miracle, in fact I would go so far as to say I would put my house on those very words being spoken (not literally of course). Think about what's being said here: "IT'S A SMALL WORLD!" Is it bollocks! It's fucking huge! Big enough to play host to the entire human race, every animal known to mankind, every type of vegetation, massive seas and oceans, huge cities with really large buildings, etc. Even stonking great porkers like Rik Waller and Vanessa Whatsername manage to squeeze in.

No, the world is in fact not remotely small, although our imagination apparently is, because that is our instinctive response, even if the encounter is only in the next town.

What we should be saying is: "Well, given the size of our planet, the number of people contained therein, and the vast diversity of social and contractual obligations we are all committed to, it is indeed amazing that coincidence or destiny has deemed our paths should cross at precisely this time and place."

Actually, that is rather a long-winded pile of bollocks, but at least it bears some resemblance to factual reality (apart from the microscopic little fact that when compared to Pluto and Jupiter it actually is a small world). We're just all too fucking lazy; if we can use a quick, cheap, crap cliché to make a point, we will. Our brains are on automatic pilot (yes, I do it too), and we just can't stop ourselves, not without a lot of practice and effort anyway.

The thing is, are you prepared to take this on board? (See, I'm doing it again, we're not on a fucking ship or a plane!) What I meant to ask is are you willing to sacrifice the soft option and start putting some thought, time and effort into the art of verbal communication?

It won't be easy, the road will be long and arduous, but with determination you can master this and become the most articulate, boring tosser on the planet. Obviously you won't bother because it is an undeniable truth that the more bollocks we talk the more colourful and interesting our language is. It would be a shame to lose what is essentially unique to our society, so this book is in serious danger of becoming the most irrelevant work of literature of all time, alongside such immortals as "Successful Motivation and Tactics in Football Management" by S.G. Ericsson.

However, as a means of interpretation for our alien invaders, it has to be the "must have" book of all time, along with the A.A. route map of the universe — "Planet Earth

(Avoiding Road Works)".

Here are loads more examples that categorically prove beyond question that a huge dollop of our everyday language is complete and utter drivel or about as appropriate as a paedophile of the year contest...

1.

HOW LONG'S A PIECE OF STRING?

Frustrated domestic resident: "Can you give me any idea when you'll be able come out and fix this leak?"

Rather arrogant and pompous, highly in demand plumber: "How long's a piece of string?"

Ah right then, so the cocky little shit who spends his time ripping off pensioners by replacing their perfectly healthy ball cocks is unwilling to give a specific response to what is in fact a perfectly reasonable question. What he is really saying is: "Given the demands on my oh so important time I am unable to specify upon which date I will grace you with my presence in order to rectify your tiresome little problem, and when I finally deem this matter of sufficient importance to justify a visit I will certainly inflate the price (so that it corresponds to what a neurosurgeon might charge for removing a tumour as big as my opinion of myself) for averting a potential fatality."

By the way, I just unravelled it and it's 13 feet 7 inches or, if you prefer metric, convert it yourself.

2.

IT'S A NO BRAINER

No, not this book, silly. "So, will I accept that fabulous job offer? Of course I will — it's a no brainer."

Erm, actually no it isn't, you see, if we were to remove that vital cerebral organ from the equation (or even your head) one has to assume that the job offer might well be withdrawn, given that a certain mental intellect would probably be required for the pursuit thereof. Unless of course the job is for a traffic warden, a Crown Court Judge, or a politician, in which case the absence of the grey sponge will make very little difference.

Correct statement: "Of course I will! This fact is indeed so blatantly obvious that the amount of thought required to make this decision is equal to the amount of thought necessary to answer an easy question without even mentioning string."

Oh, and a plumber.

3.

IT'S ONLY ME

"Hi Vera, it's only me."

"Oh, my goodness, and there I was expecting the Queen to call."

Yes, Vera's sister really has got an inferiority complex. What she should be saying is: "Hi Vera, it is I, your older sister for whom you have strong feelings of affection, slightly tempered with a degree of envy due to the fact that my Tom earns considerably more than your Bill and consequently our house is bigger."

If we really want to be picky we could argue that the person at the end of your 'phone, whoever it may be, can only ever be "me". "Hello, Vera, it's only someone else!" is just plain daft isn't it?

4.

I WON'T SAY NO

Betty to Madge: "Fancy a
cup of tea dear?"
Madge to Betty: "I won't say no."

So just say "yes", Madge. You know what? It does the same job and it's quicker. Imagine the wedding vows: "Do you take so and so [etc.]?", "I won't say I don't." Actually, perhaps you should — see number **39**.

5.

GOING ANYWHERE NICE?

"So you're off on your hols…
Going anywhere nice?"

"Actually, having spent all year looking forward to this holiday, and several months planning it, we have decided to spend a fortnight in Afghanistan's Tora Bora region in the hope of being taken hostage by Taliban fighters. It was a tough call between that and the leper colony in Somalia."

Of course you are going somewhere nice, that's the whole point of a holiday. Try this: "Work bad", "Holiday good" — get the hang of it?

Let's leave it there shall we?

6.

WORST-CASE SCENARIO

"The flight has been delayed which may mean we will miss our connection. Oh well, worst-case scenario, our luggage gets lost."

No, Mr. Traveller, it is not. The worst-case scenario is that North Korea launches a pre-emptive nuclear strike on the West and that the entire population of the western hemisphere perishes. Actually, fair do's, I suppose your luggage would be lost as well.

Correct saying: "The flight has been delayed [etc.]. I suppose that in the context of life's tragedies the possibility, indeed the likelihood, of our luggage going missing is in relative terms bearable, for if one of our children were to be kidnapped and held to ransom under threat of death, this would indeed be a greater tragedy, although I agree that this is not the first thing that springs to mind from a delayed flight."

By the way, if you have several pieces of

luggage that are not part of a matching set, herein really lies scope for a scenario involving the worst case (it might be a battered old thing on wheels).

7.

HAVE A SAFE FLIGHT

"Right then, see you in two weeks. Have a safe flight."

What kind of dumb ass thing is that to say

to someone who's about to board a plane? Everyone says it but what he or she should say is: "Whilst there is a very slight chance indeed that your plane will crash, this is highly unlikely. Therefore, in all probability you will arrive safely at your destination." As there is absolutely nothing you can do with regard to influencing the safety of your flight, unless you are actually in the cockpit or involved in the craft's maintenance, why raise the remote but daunting spectre of what everyone is trying hard not to think about: the possibility that their plane may crash? The words "Have a safe flight" do nothing other than remind people of this possibility. Next time someone says it to you just respond with, "Thanks a fucking bunch, you morbid little creep."

8.

I LAUGHED MY HEAD OFF / SPLIT MY SIDES

"So Dave tells me this joke, well it was SO funny I laughed my head off. No, really [shouldn't that be yes, really?], it was hilarious, I split my sides laughing."

Warning: whatever you do, do not, I repeat DO NOT, watch Billy Connolly live. You could end up with no head and your sides badly ripped asunder — very messy and not remotely funny. It is quite safe to watch Michael Barrymore (U.K. Gold only) or Graham Norton; I can assure you your head and sides will remain intact.

So here's what I think our giggling friend meant and should have said: "… it was SO funny that the mirth induced such an excessive degree of raucous laughter that I felt as if the interior of my cranium were about to explode, although I accept that to date there has not been a single case of cranial combustion, or sudden thoracic aperture inducement, due to the telling of a humorous or saucy tale."

Well, apart from the German General who made the über error of laughing at Adolph's muzzy and had his head blown off with a Luger. Ja! This is true.

9.

WE'LL CROSS THAT BRIDGE WHEN WE COME TO IT

Right then, so not before we come to it. Just so I understand. Okay, so that bridge which is in fact two miles away, we won't actually cross it until we are there. Got it.

What about, "I'll eat that toast when I've made it." Or, "We'll go on that holiday when the departure date arrives." Or, "I'll watch that film when it starts." I reckon there are loads more. I'll get round to them when I think of them and not before, okay?

10.

WE'LL JUST TAKE EACH GAME AS IT COMES

Utter football cliché bollocks, there are so many of them they're not worth the fucking effort — game/two halves... day/end of... parrot/sick as... robbed/we was... done good/the boy... coloured person/the lazy (Bigot Ron)... referee/blind twat, etc. Let's just do one, eh?

Interviewer: "So, Sir Alex, how do you predict the outcome of the Champions' League game against Barcelona in a fortnight?" A fair question, you might think!

Sir Alex: "Well, we have a tough game against Accrington Stanley in the F.A. Cup on Saturday and we are just taking each game as it comes."

Why can't he answer the fucking question?! We don't care about Saturday; we want to know about the big one. Perhaps he could have said: "Actually, even next Saturday is four days away and in that time fate could decree that my career or even my life is adversely affected, therefore I am only prepared to deal with questions revolving around the next five seconds of my life. I'm taking each breath as it comes."

11.

THERE'S ONE BORN EVERY MINUTE

"Oh dear, what a silly tosser [who said Sir Alex?], there's one born every minute."

One what exactly? A mental retard, that's what. Well, actually statistics suggest that a relatively low percentage of babies are born with such brain defects. I can't be bothered looking up the exact numbers so I would guess that "one" is actually only born every seven and a half minutes or even longer. So that saying is total bollocks.

Correct saying: "Yes, he is a complete fucking idiot insomuch as he has just paid me well over the odds for this battered old Vauxhall Victor, but he is in fact not the only fool by any means, although I can't be specific with regard to the birth ratios of the cerebrally challenged and the hyper gullible relative to commonly termed normal folk."

12.

THERE'S NOTHING WORSE THAN. . .

"So John, you're in a rush and you can't locate your car keys. There's nothing worse than that is there?"

Oh really, so there you are fumbling around the house, being late for the cinema or whatever. Your neighbour swings by, sees you in a rage, and offers this utterly hopeless and grossly inaccurate piece of linguistic dog shit.

I could go to town on this (no I couldn't, I can only go to town on a bus or a bike) but come on, I ask you — "nothing worse than"? How about having your pubic hair removed with a blowtorch? That's worse. What else? Oh yeah, treading on a hedgehog with your bare feet, that's much worse. And there are loads of others. Utter bollocks.

Correct version: "Isn't it a trifle inconvenient when you lose something and the consequence is that you may miss the trailers? Of course, the cinema may burn down with you and your family trapped inside. There really is nothing worse than that."

13.

I'M MEETING MYSELF COMING BACK

"I just don't know how I'm going to get all this done. I'm meeting myself coming back."

So you're a bit busy, you've had to do several things at once and now you've somehow split into two people and, I suppose, inevitably, seeing as you're in the one house or wherever, you bump into your doppelgänger. This is a great example of the kind of total bollocks that we churn out on a daily basis.

Correct version: "Due to my own lack of organisational skills and time management I fear I may be running a little late with this task."

If, however, you have an identical twin or work in the house of mirrors at the fairground I suppose (one of) you could argue a case.

14.

YOU COULD GET HIT BY A BUS

"Oh stop worrying! You could get hit by a bus."

Well, yes, of course you could. But to use this drivel in the context of telling someone not to worry about, for example, their smoking, drinking or drugs habit that has caused spiralling financial problems is truly crap. The odds of them dying from their excessive lifestyle are in fact astronomically higher than the chances of them being hit by a bus.

Statistically, you have a one in five million chance of being hit by a bus. In fact, the chances of you actually catching a bus are about one in a thousand in certain areas. Oh, and forget all that rubbish about waiting ages then two turning up, it doesn't happen — okay?

Correct version: "I suggest that you take a rational view on your survival chances by weighing up the risk factors of your over indulgences balanced against the obvious pleasure you derive therein, thus mitigating your concern possibly to the detriment of balanced judgment and thereby rendering the bus analogy redundant."

15.

YOU CAN'T TURN BACK THE CLOCK

"No, you shouldn't have acted like a prick. Unfortunately you can't turn back the clock."

Just cast your mind back (as if your brain were on the end of a fishing line) to those Saturday nights/Sunday mornings every late

October. You are, in fact, compelled to turn back the clocks, and what's more it's very simple. Unless, of course, you possess one of those awkward little fuckers with tiny screws at the back which need completely dismantling thanks to some twat of a clock designer who lives by the creed "You can't turn back the clocks" and who has made it his mission in life to prove it.

Obviously, with the exception of the little shithead just mentioned, the clear fact is that of course you can turn back the clock. You can also do this by travelling to different countries where for some incomprehensible reason they choose to have their own time zones.

Correct saying: "I'm afraid you have completely fucked up and sadly you are now stuck with the consequences as the damage your actions have caused is irreversible. By the way, don't forget the clocks go back tomorrow night."

16.

I'VE BEEN FEELING UNDER PAR

"Oh dear, sniff, sniff, I really have been feeling under par lately."

Have you now? Well, good for you. Because you clearly fail to grasp the concept of the term "under par" in its correct place, which is in regard to your golf score. It isn't that difficult: par is what you should score (gross off scratch or net off a handicap). The whole point is to shoot as low as possible therefore to be under par is in fact fucking brilliant because golf is a bastard of a game!

Got that? Okay, so you feel a bit shitty, try this: "Oh God, I feel loads over par." In fact if you've got a bad cold you could throw in a few bogies and be really clever.

Footnote: If you said you felt "under the weather", I still wouldn't be happy because you are seldom over the weather, but I would let it go, just.

17.

YOU COULDN'T MAKE IT UP

"And then this extraordinary thing happened which you may find hard to believe. I'm telling you, you couldn't make it up."

So something very amazing has happened, in relative terms to your otherwise uninspiring life. Let's think now, what could it be? What about this: you went for a walk and saw a spaceship. Little green men jumped out and asked for directions to Pluto saying they were lost. When you said you had no idea because you weren't from round here they started sneezing and suddenly they all turned into aardvarks.

Well, you couldn't make it up, could you? Well guess what, I just fucking well did, in fact I could make up just about anything. So there, you COULD make it up no matter how unlikely an event, and what's more I've just proved it.

Correct saying: "Whilst man's imagination could indeed stretch to fabrication of the events I am about to relate, the following is nonetheless hard to believe and pushes credibility to (and possibly beyond) breaking point."

18.

YOU COULD HAVE KNOCKED ME DOWN WITH A FEATHER

"So there he was, large as life. I thought he'd died years ago. You could have knocked me down with a feather."

Fucking hell! You must be light, or it's the world's biggest feather, perhaps from an ostrich. So, you've just had a real shock, let's say your great granny has given birth to quads and you've just heard the news.

What's so wrong with: "Well, given that the old bird is 94, I must say that came as a major surprise, especially as she had a hysterectomy in her forties."

If you feel you must make the point in a more dramatic way then what about: "You could have knocked me down with a steam roller."

My flat mate got run over with a steamroller, by the way.

19.

SHE WEARS HER HEART ON HER SLEEVE

"Oh yes, she's such an emotional person, she wears her heart on her sleeve."

No she does not, well not unless she has had the world's first external heart transplant which I suppose might just be possible by cleverly joining up nerves and arteries from your arm and attaching your heart to them. It would be very messy and the lady in question would never be able to wear a sleeveless dress. There would probably also be a huge risk of cardiac infection, in fact the more I think about it the less inclined I am to accept the possibility.

At a very long push I might just accept "She wears her heart on her arm" but I'm not happy about that.

There are loads of other "heart" sayings: "You're all heart." (So no lungs, liver or kidneys then.); "Have a heart." (Surely they do.); "Let's have a heart-to-heart."

(A mouth-to-ear would be better.); "His heart's in the right place." (That's lucky for him.)

Look, the heart is a major organ stuck somewhere in the chest, near all them ribs and lungs. It's there for a reason — don't fuck with it.

Oh dear, the major organ of the body is chasing me with a knife; I'm having a heart attack… see what I mean. Utter bollocks.

20.

WHEN YOU'VE SEEN ONE YOU'VE SEEN THEM ALL

"So then his towel slipped down and I saw his willy. I wasn't impressed; when you've seen one you've seen them all."

Really, so given that this term frequently seems to refer to a female viewing a male sex organ, are we to believe that the onlooker has in fact seen every penis in the world? I think not, for it would take at least five years of staking out every male urinal on earth, suitably disguised or concealed, and one has to assume that one would eventually get arrested well before completion of said task.

Correct terminology: "I was unimpressed with the sight of his todger as it differs only marginally in both form and dimension from a vast array of todgers. This is an assumption based on the few I have seen. However, I must accept that it is conceivable that there may be in existence willies which differ monumentally to those I have actually clapped eyes on."

The term bollocks is indeed appropriate for this linguistic faux pas.

21.

ROME WASN'T BUILT IN A DAY

"Just be patient; Rome wasn't built in a day you know."

No?! Well I fucking never. But I suppose

Sydney, Moscow, New York and London were. Not to mention Liverpool, Athens, Tokyo (I have to accept here that certain Japanese cities were in fact unbuilt in a day), Paris, Benidorm… Actually, Benidorm might have been built in a day.

So you're trying to tell us to be patient; that some things take a little longer. Well what's wrong with: "Earth wasn't created in six days." Actually, it might have been. Or scaling that down to: "My house wasn't built in 0.00005 seconds." It's a total bollocks of verbal overkill, given that when the plans for Rome were submitted in 1066, the schedule for on time completion thereby avoiding penalties was in fact three months, two weeks, four days, 12 hours and 17.5 minutes. So not a day then!

22.

BIG ISSUE, PLEASE

Man trying to sell you the Big Issue: "Big Issue, please."

This is about as good an example of sheer grammatical bollocks as you're ever likely to hear. Listen, you homeless folks, this is how it works in our language: "Cup of tea, please" means I haven't got one and I'd like one. "Pint of lager, please" — ditto. "Big Issue, please"? Next time someone screams this in my lugs, I'm just going to reply, "You've already got one." Enough said.

23.

EVERY CLOUD HAS
A SILVER LINING

" So, Rupert, I believe you have just
lost your job, the wife's walked out and
you're H.I.V. positive. Never mind,
every cloud has a silver lining. "

Right, so every bit of shit that comes our way
actually carries with it a big dollop of good

fortune. Try telling that to a quadriplegic who can just about move his or her eyeballs on a good day. They'd probably smack you in the face; at least they would if they could. I guess they'd just have to glare at you.

If we're going to be pedantic, which let's face it is the whole purpose of this book, what we should be saying is: "There are indeed occasions where destiny sends misfortune our way and through this unenviable, desperate and often heartbreaking time sometimes there comes an unexpected benefit. However, most times shit is shit, period."

24.

A WATCHED POT NEVER BOILS

" It's no good sitting there watching those new motorway lanes being built. A watched pot never boils. "

Fucking does, try it. Just because staring at the kettle when you're gasping for a cup of tea may seem to drag on somewhat, please understand that this is an illusionary perception that denies reality.

I accept here that my motorway example is stretching things a little in trying to compare 26 months of snail-paced labour to the two minutes a kettle takes to boil water.

Correct saying: "If your life is so dull that you have nothing better to do than gawp at that kettle, time will indeed seem to pass more slowly than say the five minutes of freeview on Red Hot Dutch, which, conversely, passes far too quickly."

25.

YOU CAN'T HAVE IT BOTH WAYS

Really, well just ask any bi-sexual person, if you know any. Actually you probably do know some without knowing you know some if you know what I mean. It's a bit like the cake one (see **32**) but the cake one is non sexual and this one isn't.

26.

HE'S GOT HIS HEAD IN THE CLOUDS

" I don't know… [sigh] that lad's such a dreamer. He's got his head in the clouds, you know. "

If you're Peter Crouch, that may be the case. As for the rest of us, no way. But hang on, doesn't this really infer that he has ideas above his station? (Well, is it a train station, a bus station or what?) Or that he's up his own arse? Well that's almost a physical impossibility, I know when I tried... er, anyway, it's just not possible, you can't have it both ways you know.

Correct version: "I'm sure his aspirations outweigh the potential he has thus far displayed with regard to his ambitions for future success." Alternatively: "Dream on, bollock brains."

27.

I'M NOT BEING FUNNY BUT...

" I'm not being funny but if she carries on drinking like that Auntie Edna will be dead in two years. "

Well isn't it a good job you prefixed your gloomy statement of observation with that particular clarification... Otherwise it could easily have been misconstrued as an attempt at causing merriment.

You should have said: "Given the rather morbid assessment I am about to deliver with regard to the ongoing survival chances of this particular alcohol-loving close relative, I wish to make it abundantly clear that this prognosis is delivered with due acknowledgment to the gravity of the situation." Or: "If the drunken old bat doesn't stop getting bladdered she'll pop her clogs soon, and I'm not joking."

28.

I'M OVER THE MOON

> "Ooh, I'm so happy. Something really good has happened and I'm over the moon."

Okay, let's assume the American lunar landing wasn't a hoax. Yes, you could argue a case for Neil Armstrong and his mates coming out with that one. For the rest of us who remain on planet Earth… no way, Hose A.

It has become one of those after game footy person clichés, boring as fuck. What's so wrong with: "Yes, it was a fine draw for our boys, and I am especially pleased with the contribution I personally made by scoring one goal which, even though in the great scheme of sporting occasions it merely ranks with a reasonably good Chester Barnes ping pong serve, I celebrated with the manic, dramatic enthusiasm of an Olympic gold medal winning athlete. I am indeed in a state of cerebral ecstasy hitherto not experienced other than after the birth of my baby daughter which remains top of my list of all time nice things wot happened.

Well that and twatting United's centre half last week."

I suppose you could argue a case for the following: "I got really drunk and flashed my arse the other day. At first I felt embarrassed but now I'm over the moon."

29.

YOU'RE A LONG TIME DEAD

" You know, you might as well
enjoy yourself while you can,
you're a long time dead. "

Oh dear, this one is loaded. Let's think
about what is being implied here. The
speaker seems to be assuming that there
is no afterlife and that, once deceased,
your mortal remains exist in relation to

space and time for an undefined period, this being "a long time". This may be so, however, if, as many believe, we should be laying the foundations for an onward journey into the heavens or wherever, then it leaves itself wide open to contradiction, albeit based on supposition and faith rather than hard evidence.

Perhaps we should hedge our bets with this one. How about: "Whilst there may be some justification for pleasurable indulgence during our far too short existence in human form, perhaps it would be wise to contemplate alternative, spiritual endings, bearing in mind that we may be subjected to behavioural judgment, from a higher power, at the end of our journey."

Oh fuck it, just have fun.

30.

YOU CAN'T TAKE IT WITH YOU

"You might as well spend it all while you can, you can't take it with you."

Bollocks you can't. You can get quite

a wodge into a coffin. Don't leave it for the brats; they'll only piss it up the wall. Anyway, imagine getting to the Pearly Gates and being asked for £5 admission fee. You'd have to say, "Sorry St. Peter. They said I couldn't take it with me and I haven't any money." "Well fuck off then," St Peter would have to say and who could blame him?

Of course it might cost a grand to get in, that's the problem, nobody knows. In fact, to be safe, you really do need to take it all with you.

So that's sorted that one then.

31.

BETTER STOP AND ASK FOR DIRECTIONS

Passenger/Navigator: "Oh dear,
I think we are lost. You'd better
stop and ask for directions."

Brilliant, there you are doing 45 mph in a
30 mph zone. Haven't a clue where you are.
You are definitely going to need to ask for

directions, probably off a passing pedestrian. And in fact I can't argue with this one, apart from stating the blindingly obvious, that you'll have to STOP first.

I suppose you could slow down enough for a jogger to keep pace and give directions as you're moving but he's likely to run into a lamp post and hurt his head so, yes, stopping is good.

32.

YOU CAN'T HAVE YOUR CAKE AND EAT IT

"So, Mabel, you met this gorgeous guy in the pub but he turned out to be gay. Oh well, you can't have your cake and eat it."

Whoa! Let's nail this one straight away. Anyone been into the bakers? Did you buy a cake? Did you eat it? You DID! Well you fucking shouldn't have, apparently.

As for Mabel and her shirt lifter friend, what's cake got to do with it anyway? Unless it's a fruitcake, of course. Ah, now that makes perfect sense. Hang on, I thought you said this one was non sexual — liar!

Correct statement for all other cake scenarios: "Blah blah etc., oh well, you can't expect to eat the cake, er no, buy cake and, er hang on, have cake and make crumbs, er not make crumbs." Oh heck, struggling here, thought this one would be a piece of cake.

33.

WHAT, NONE AT ALL?

"Have we had any callers enquiring about the car I'm selling, darling? None? What, none at all?"

A beauty this one, like there are degrees of noneness. No fucker called. Now get over it.

34.

THAT'S THE STORY OF MY LIFE

"So there I was, stuck in this fucking broken lift, with the most boring arse'ole on the planet. And I was late for my stamp collectors meeting. Oh well, that's the story of my life."

Is it really? So your entire life has thus far

been spent in a lift with the same person, from the day you were born up until now. No wonder this person seems boring, the world's greatest raconteur would seem boring after a lifetime together in a lift.

Yes we know that's not what actually happened, so why imply through dialogue that it is? It's probably accounted for ten whole minutes of your life, which, even being generous assuming you had David Dimbleby in there, would only seem like two hours.

You should have said: "… stamp collectors meeting [etc.]. Oh well, that's a rather insignificant incident appertaining to a relatively trivial portion of my existence, barely worthy of mention."

Understand this: the story of your life is a fucking biography, auto or otherwise, and unless you're a little bit famous and have something more interesting to tell than your lift story, it ain't gonna happen, okay?

35.

HOW DID YOU SLEEP?

Well, actually, I took my clothes off, having first seen to my toilet needs, then climbed into my slumber vessel. I put myself into a horizontal position and closed my eyes, then after a bit of shuffling about I drifted into a state of sufficient relaxation for my conscious mind to transform into a state of nocturnal cerebral disengagement. I remained thus for about eight hours, constantly shifting from one dream pattern to the next, during which time I imagined myself indulging in acts of lewdness with a variety of nubile females.

When I woke up I had a stiffy. Answer your question?

36.

I SLEPT LIKE A LOG

Well my todger was like a log (see number **35**). No seriously, I lay there all night and didn't so much as move a twig. This would be how a log would sleep, yeah?

37.

TAKE CARE

"Well, nice to see you.
Bye, bye, take care."

Oh yes, do take care, be sure not to jump in front of that bus (so it CAN happen), or leap out of that top floor window. And be sure not to go to any war zones where you may be taken hostage or even killed, on holiday for instance (going anywhere nice?). And please don't stick your finger into an electric socket, and er, oh yes, don't go stroking any tigers at the zoo, etc...

Whilst I thank you for your concern, I feel I have enough life experience and common sense to avoid all of these things mentioned and many others without the benefit of your well intended but totally obvious and rather condescending advice.

What you should say is: "Bye, bye... Try not to get eaten by a shark, but statistically you probably won't. By the way, do enjoy your holiday swimming off the Barrier Reef."

… bum, bum, bum, bum, bum, bum…
(that's a shark creeping up, nothing to do
with your botty)…

38.

YOU CAN'T BEAT A NICE CUP OF TEA

Oh dear, just where do we start? So, basically
a cup of common or garden (common yes,
but garden?) tea receives the supreme award,

it's the pinnacle of ecstasy, the ultimate pleasurable experience. Yup, the little cuppa actually wards off competition from all those big boys like er, sex, footy, getting pissed, watching Corrie, etc.

Yes, I know it's only a figure of speech, like all the others, but as I keep saying, it's a totally fucking wrong number.

Try this instead: "Ah, yes, very nice. You know I have to say that drinking this cup of tea has heightened my sense of enjoyment by merely the tiniest percentage, which in all honesty is about what you'd expect from such a simple and everyday routine act."

And by the way, it wouldn't have taken so long if you hadn't been staring at that fucking kettle…

39.

I DO
(or I won't say no — see no. 4)

Oh yes, the shortest of the lot and yet the most loaded. Basically, the priest or whoever asks you if you are prepared to spend your entire life putting up with and having sex with the same person. Because everyone's watching, you ain't gonna say "no" are you? You haven't got the balls, even though you know you are already lusting after her sister who you've just noticed for the first time actually looks quite shaggable all dolled up in her bridesmaid's outfit.

Correct saying: "In relation to the level of expectation and the romantically based motives of any couple standing here, bearing in mind our understandably clouded judgment due to being in a heightened emotional state, one is bound to answer in the affirmative. However, this in no way denies the irrefutable statistical evidence which categorically suggests that this arrangement is in all probability temporary due to our mutual and insatiable desire to find our way into someone else's pants at our earliest convenience." In other words: "I doubt it."

40.

IS THE GLASS HALF FULL OR HALF EMPTY?

For God's sake, what bleeding difference does it make? Yes, I know it's supposed to be a way of differentiating between optimism and pessimism, so fucking say, "Is it looking good or bad?" It's actually quicker.

To justify the inclusion of this particular linguistic bollocks, let's just explore this a little. Glass starts empty, you fill it therefore it's full. You drink (empty) half so it is now half empty. On the other hand if you only half fill it in the first place it is clearly half full. That's how easy it is. If you drink three quarters of it, it is therefore three quarters empty, or is it a quarter full? Oh shit, I'm confused now.

See the trouble you've caused? If only you'd said, "I was just wondering how you currently perceive this situation in terms of positivity or negativity, perhaps we could discuss this over a half of lager. Barman, could you please put half of lager into this pint glass so that it's half empty... Oh bollocks..."

41.

IT NEVER RAINS (BUT IT POURS)

"And then, to top it all, the cat ran off and the cake, which I could have had but not eaten, exploded in the oven. I dunno, it never rains but it pours."

I want you to look outside, now. Tell me is it drizzling? No? Well did it drizzle yesterday? Come on, we all know that this is about as inaccurate a load of verbal plop as you could imagine.

So basically, apparently it never rains (therefore it is always totally bone dry) but it absolutely pisses down (therefore it is always totally soaking wet). You can't have it both ways; I think we've already dealt with this, can you?

Even the correct interpretation of this ("Things never just go a bit wrong do they? It's always a complete fuck up.") is pure tripe. Of course, things sometimes go a bit wrong, like when I forgot to video the football once and got some cookery shite on the box. Look, it does sometimes just drizzle, as sure as...

42.

AS SURE AS EGGS IS EGGS. . .

"Yes, we're off on holiday tomorrow. We're bound to forget something, sure as eggs is eggs."

(Glass half empty or what?) First off, eggs isn't eggs is they? Eggs, being in the plural in fact are eggs. Not enough that this is grammatically a pile of pooh, it also hits a very loud discordant note in terms of a descriptive narrative. How would "sure as hens is hens" sound, or "bananas is bananas"? Actually I quite like that, but it won't catch on sure as elephants is elephants.

All right, I admit it, it's hard to beat an eggs (is eggs). You could try scrambled eggs; it's worth taking the whisk. Okay, really bad joke, I'm sure you agree. Ah yes, great minds…

43.

GREAT MINDS THINK ALIKE

Er, actually they don't. Einstein supported Bolton Wanderers and Shakespeare supported Plymouth Argyle. All right, I'm being literal again. Here's the scenario:

"Gosh, Hillary, fancy bumping in to you [optional — "It's a small world"] at Blockbuster and us both selecting Bridget Jones, The Edge of Reason — great minds think alike."

So the fact that Hillary and her friend have both chosen the Bridget Jones sequel somehow elevates their mental status to genius level. I would have thought the exact opposite was true.

She should be saying: "Gosh Hillary, it would appear that you are as intellectually shallow as I am, as proven by the fact that we have simultaneously opted to watch the latest Hugh Grant chick flick pile of cack. Aren't we a sad pair of old trollops?! And, it ISN'T a small world either, unless you compare it to Jupiter or Pluto."

44.

I'D GIVE MY RIGHT ARM FOR. . .

"Oh yes, I'm determined to become the world skipping champion, I'd give my right arm for that."

Might make it just a tad difficult old boy (or girl), given that both limbs are an intrinsic part of the act of skipping. And why is it never the left arm? A trifle limbist, I fear, or is it leftist? As for the leg, it doesn't even get a sniff, hang on, legs can't smell (feet can though).

I think he's trying to convey the following message: "... I'd certainly sacrifice something precious in the pursuit of my skipping dream, however I must specify that this must in no way involve the amputation, or loss by any means, of body parts which are essential to my quest. At a push I would give my left ear lobe for this."

By the way, if you plan to skip lunch you'll need a very long piece of spaghetti, as well as two arms.

45.

MY WIFE DOESN'T UNDERSTAND ME

"I don't normally pick up girls at bus shelters, but I'm going through a tough time; my wife doesn't understand me."

Spoken after a long wait for a prostitute, and then along come two at once.

So presumably your wife is Latvian and

speaks no English. Or you're always so pissed and mumble so badly that she can't possibly make out a word you're saying.

What you mean is that your wife is struggling to come to terms with the fact that she married a horny little shit who lusts after anything with tits and who views monogamy with about as much relish as Robbie Coltrane does his weight watchers' diet sheet.

Correct translation: "My wife thinks I'm working late because I constantly lie to her about my whereabouts whilst I'm busy pursuing my hobby of shagging cheap whores like you due to the fact I am so fat and ugly I couldn't possibly attract a woman in my own right. Have you got change of a fiver, and can I have it both ways, please?"

46.

YOU CAN NEVER SAY NEVER

T.V. journalist: "So, Mr. Fading Actor, after three mediocre years in the nation's number one soap you are leaving to pursue your

Hollywood dream. When it all turns to rat shit will you come crawling back begging to be reinstated in Corrie?"

Mr. Head in the Clouds (Peter Crouch?), totally deluded, dream-on-sunshine, fading actor: "Oh, I wouldn't have thought so, but then again, you can never say never."

Hang on, bullock brain, you just did say it — twice. Here is an amazing example of a self-contradicting, hyperbolic, logic twisting, metaphorical, mumbo jumbo sized piece of total and utter nonsensical excrement.

I think our lacklustre, head-beyond-the-clouds-and-on-the-edge-of-outer-space, self-proclaiming-would-be-luvvie-superstar is trying to say: "Given the amount of fan mail I received after one particular Christmas episode of Albion Market where I actually had slightly more than a walk on and fart part (five letters, three of which came from family members), and the fact that a decrepit old bat in the Co-op once asked me to sign her support bandage, I feel that I am now worthy of elevation to an altogether higher level of respect and I await the deluge of offers which will inevitably precede my permanent move to L.A. Failing that, I will be only too happy to play an ugly sister at Bridlington Rep."

47.

I WISH I HAD A POUND FOR EVERY TIME I'VE SAID THAT

Man in pub: "You know what, you can't beat a good old pint [not a cup of tea then?]. I wish I had a pound for every time I've said that…"

Unfortunately, it doesn't quite work like that. Firstly, from whom is the pound due? Who on Earth (as opposed to who on Jupiter, which is significantly larger than Earth) is going to accept responsibility for not only keeping count of the number of times you said whatever it is you wished you had a pound for every time you said it? And secondly, who in their right mind (as opposed to their wrong mind) is going to volunteer to make such payments?

It's a tricky one from both a moral and legal standpoint, given that the burden of proof of responsibility rests with the person to whom the pound, for every time they said whatever it is they wished to get a pound for, is payable. They'd laugh it out of court, and what's more, how would you predetermine exactly what it is you wish to nominate as the thing you would say for which a pound would be payable every time you said it?

I really don't think you'd pull it off, but there again, you can never say never.

48.

IT TAKES ALL SORTS TO MAKE A WORLD

Same man in pub: "See that weird old bugger over there, with the Bovril flavoured Pimms? He collects Pot Noodle tubs. By 'eck [you'll have gathered he's a Northerner] it takes all sorts…"

Well, yes, I suppose it does as far as planet

Earth is concerned. However, if, as some folks believe, there exist indigenous species of life form on other planets, each with an identical genetic make up, then you'd have to dispute this statement, strongly.

However, in the context of this world, I accept that we are a varied blend of black, white, male, female, yellow, big, small, smart, stupid, etc. Therefore, if we replace the word "a" with the word "this" we could theoretically eliminate this ever so slightly erroneous statement from our dung heap. By the way, let's not forget how small this world is.

49.

IT'S NO USE FLOGGING A DEAD HORSE

Sad, dejected ex-boyfriend: "That's the fifth time Brenda's chucked me, I ain't asking her back again — it's no use flogging a dead horse."

Whoa boy, easy in the saddle there, rein it in a little! Should you be fortunate enough to have in your possession a recently expired member of the equine species I would certainly argue a case for the merits and significant commercial benefits of flogging it to, for example, a glue manufacturer, or perhaps a strange sexual deviant with a penchant for bestial necrophilia.

So while our poor, rejected and dejected ex-boyfriend pontificates on the hopelessness of his relationship prospects with Brenda, it's really no excuse for coming out with such an obviously inaccurate, and commercially naive, statement.

Simple alternative: "Oh well, looks

like Brenda's off the shagging rota for the foreseeable."

50.

FANTASTIC!

Lady desk clerk at car rental booth: "So, Mr. Tompkins, if you'd just like to sign [...your life away!] on the dotted line."

Mr. Tompkins duly obliges, thereby committing himself to the loan of a Ford

Mondeo for three days. Lady desk clerk (I guarantee this): "Fantastic!" (or possibly "Brilliant!", it doesn't matter which.)

So apparently Mrs. Desk Clerk, in an act of grossly exaggerated grovelling praise, thinks that Mr. Tompkins' signing of his name merits a display of admiration normally reserved for someone who has perhaps performed a feat somewhat more challenging. Unless, of course, in an outrageous display of bravado and exhibitionism, Mr. Tompkins has in fact removed his shoe and sock and performed the signing act with the pen between his toes, and perhaps also given the ancestral lineage of the Tompkins family dating back 500 years, and all of this translated into Japanese. Oh yes, now that would be fantastic, if a little time consuming.

She merely had to say: "Well, that wasn't too difficult was it, seeing as how you've probably been doing it for most of your life. Unless of course you have recently changed your name from Johnson, in which case well done, but not really fantastic!"

51.

IT WAS NOTHING TO WRITE HOME ABOUT

"Yes, we did go to that new Venezuelan restaurant in town. It was okay but, to be honest, it was nothing to write home about."

A strange one this, as our diner friend seems to be using this exaggerated piece of bollock lingo to convey to his chum that the restaurant was just okay (again, not only quicker but also more to the point).

So let's assume that the restaurant was in fact superb, in which case our munching mate would have been busy putting pen to paper no doubt, as follows:

Dear everyone in our house,

Although I know that we will all return from the Thai restaurant at precisely the same time as this correspondence arrives, unless I post it which would be silly, and that in fact we will all be aware of the contents prior to sight of such communication,

I just wanted to inform all of you (us) that the restaurant in which we all dined tonight was in fact quite fantastic, and totally worthy of this dispatch. In fact, the only negative was that for dessert I ordered cake that, although presented to me, I was not allowed to consume.

Yours truly (honest, I'm not lying),

Me

P.S. But then you (and I) already know this.

52.

HE'S GOT A SWEET TOOTH

Woman to neighbour, regarding hubby George's eating habits: "Oh yes, my George enjoys his pud [which is why he's a fat bastard], he's got a sweet tooth you know."

Well no, actually we didn't know until you told us, but here's the question. If he's got a sweet tooth why bother with pudding? Why not just lick his tooth and derive endless taste bud pleasure from that presumably infinite phenomenon which is "the sugared fang"?

It must be like having a permanent sweetie in your gob, how nice! And if the nasty dentist ever did extract it, well lucky old George could simply take it home and suck on it every time he felt a sweet fix coming on. Or if he was just having a filling perhaps he could ask for marzipan or treacle flavour.

Yes, you may well know what George's wife was suggesting, but I bet our alien friends would be confused — I certainly am, quite literally. But that's another story.

EPILOGUE

I think I'll save the next 52 bollock-brained sayings (that's one a week for the next year) for the follow-up book; we know it's going to happen sure as eggs is eggs. Enough is enough (obviously) and it's no use flogging a dead horse. When will it happen? How long is a piece of string? Let's cross that bridge when we come to it and take each book as it comes. Worst-case scenario, this one won't even be published — well, you can't have your cake and eat it can you?

I hope you've derived a modicum of pleasure from this collection of linguistic nonsense, it's all tongue in cheek and of course I wouldn't even dream of trying to diminish any of the wonderfully idiosyncratic metaphors of our language, but I do feel sorry for our alien friends when they finally arrive (if they're not here already, as if Pluto isn't big enough for them). They just ain't gonna get it!

Anyway, that's yer lot from me for now, I've enjoyed it and I hope you have too, and I wish I had a pound for every time I've said that.

Professor R. Lingo
2008

Footnote:

Thanks are due to the entire human race, but particularly the British, for their unique and unlimited ability to be able to waffle, spout rubbish, talk shite and generally give our language its own inimitable sense of identity. And you can't say fairer than that — hang on, I just did!

MORE BOLLOCKS
(for another time)

1. The shit's gonna hit the fan

2. Ooh, your baby looks just like you

3. Come on, it's not the end
   of the world

4. They broke the mould when they
   made him

5.   How was your meal?

6.   Oh, you've gotta laugh haven't you?

7.   May I help you?

8.   He's worth a bob or two

9.   I haven't got a bean

10. So, what happened to summer?

11. I won't be a moment

12. That's all you ever talk about

13. I could have died

14. Shit happens

15. Two heads are better than one

16. You've got me over a barrel

17. It's like looking for a needle

    in a haystack

18. It's raining cats and dogs

19. You scratch my back and I'll scratch yours

20. Got out of bed on the wrong side

21. Fortune favours the brave

22. Only the good die young

23. I think he's lost the plot

24. The sky's the limit

25. You're joking

26. He's got a twinkle in his eye

27. It's like watching paint dry

28. She's not been herself lately

29. She's no oil painting

30. He's worth a small fortune

31. Don't beat yourself up about it

32. Not a sausage

33. Make a pig's ear of it

34. Left high and dry

35. Money for old rope

36. Push the boat out

37. A square meal

38. Sent to Coventry

39. He's a dark horse

40. How the other half lives

41. Ignorance is bliss

42. My ears are burning

43. It's in the lap of the Gods

44. Don't move a muscle

45. She's the apple of his eye

46. Yes and no

47. Something and nothing

48. It is and it isn't

49. To die for

50. A different kettle of fish

51. I'll fight him tooth and nail

52. Just gonna jump in the bath

www.crombiejardine.com

Bollocks